passion play [2010]
oberammergau

THE PASSION PLAY
2010
OBERAMMERGAU

EDITED BY THE
Community of Oberammergau

DIRECTOR
Christian Stückl

STAGE-SET AND COSTUME DESIGN
Stefan Hageneier

DRAMATURGY
Otto Huber

PHOTOGRAPHY
Brigitte Maria Mayer

PRESTEL Munich · Berlin · London · New York

"WHO DO YOU THINK THAT I AM?"

This question that Jesus asked his disciples also provides us in Oberammergau with our greatest challenge every ten years. Of course everybody can think of some words to answer this question: the one who was beaten, scourged and crucified or the Redeemer, the Saviour, the Forgiver of Sins. Our heads are full of images and most of these have been influenced by the 19th-century Nazarene movement of German Romantic painters: the shepherd with the lamb on his shoulders, long, generally blond hair and, of course, sandals. These are words that I have heard and images I have had in my head ever since I was a child, and even today I have my problems with them. Even today I ask myself: who was or is he really?

During my search for him I came across the young Jew, known in Hebrew-Aramaic as Jeshua, about whom we can read that, at the tender age of twelve, when in Jerusalem with his parents, asked questions in the temple that a child of his age does not normally ask. His parents who had lost him in the crowd, found him in the temple among the learned, listening to them. He soon got into conversation and started to ask questions. In the Gospel of Luke it says: "And all that heard him were astonished at his understanding and answers" (Luke 2:47). Even at an early age, even though we know nothing about his youth, he seems to be filled with great ideas. The message of the Kingdom of God, a kingdom that is marked by God's gift of love to the world, a love that offers forgiveness and is there for everyone, is at the heart of his proclamation. This idea impels him to be among people. And with increasing clarity he seeks out a new path to follow. The words "Repent ye" become the central message of his teachings. Jesus expresses most concisely the need to rethink radically in his Sermon on the Mount, when he says that, for him, there is no commandment more important than that of love, of a love of God and other people. But what is so special about his words? Haven't we heard them thousands of times before and haven't they become devoid of meaning?

Jesus, the young Jew, was speaking in an Israel governed by Rome, in a world full of social contradictions based on suppression and exploitation. The ruling Sadducees cooperated with the Romans who quashed any uprisings. Pontius Pilate, as we now know today, had countless insurgents crucified – the priests themselves being predominantly concerned about their own image. Those who didn't obey were disciplined. The people yearned to be liberated from Roman oppression, from heavy taxes and slavery; they yearned for a king, a Messiah on the throne of the Jews. It was in such a world, in such a situation that Jesus of Nazareth spoke the unconditional commandment of loving one's neighbour, a commandment that is valid for all, for beggars, slaves and prostitutes, as well as for the much-hated Roman soldiers and their commander Pontius Pilate, who had thousands of Jews executed. Jesus' proclamation was

for a new image of mankind. For him, we are all equal in God's eyes and our lives will be judged by how we treat our neighbours. Jesus' call to a radical rethinking, his "Repent ye", is a call to put a stop to hatred and counter-hatred, violence and counter-violence.

He speaks to the priests as a believer and a Jew: "Hear, O Israel; The Lord our God is one Lord; / …there is one God; and there is none other but he: And to love him with all the heart, and with all the understanding, and with all the soul, and with all the strength, and to love his neighbour as himself, is more than all whole burnt offerings and sacrifices" (Mark 12:29, 32–33). He makes it quite clear to them that rituals cannot buy God's love and that it is not just a question of keeping to traditional rules and regulations. With the words: "You have omitted the weightier matters of the law that God has given us through Moses, judgment, mercy, and faith" (see Matthew 23:23) he banishes the thought from all those who believed he wanted to distance himself from Moses and the Commandments or who believed that he and his disciples wanted to proclaim their own teachings. The powers-that-be at that time considered his words an attack on their position. Jesus clashed more and more with the authorites – a clash that ultimately led to his death.

For me, Jesus is not a suffering servant of God, not a sacrificial lamb. For me, Jesus is an argumentative young Jew who was nailed to the cross for pro-claiming a message that is still valid today. These thoughts were the driving force behind our revision of the text for the Passion Play for 2010. We want to show a Jesus who, with unflinching stead-fastness, stood for the belief he had in his god who is also the God of Abraham, the God of Isaac and the God of Jacob – namely the God of the Jews.

Over a period of many months, more than 2,000 amateur actors, singers and musicians from Oberammergau have been rehearsing; hundreds of new costumes have been made and a new stage-set built. For everyone in Oberammergau, 2010 revolves around the 41st Passion Play season. After all the effort that the people of Oberammergau have been proud to demonstrate over 376 years – since making the vow that launched the Passion Play tradition in 1633 – we hope that something of the spirit comes across as described by St. Luke at the end of his gospel: "And all the people that came together to that sight, beholding the things which were done, smote their breasts, and returned" (Luke 23:48).

Christian Stückl
Director, April 2010

THE ENTRY INTO JERUSALEM

The Oberammergau **Passion Play** opens by focussing on humankind's desire to find salvation and the hope offered through Jesus Christ.

Adam and Eve bemoan the fate of those who turn away from God: "Lord, where art thou! We are lost, with no shelter, destined to die."

From the very beginning, the life of Jesus Christ falls under a different sign. He is borne by God. He exudes an energy that enables him to do good deeds. And, in his words and actions, he seeks to convey to his fellow men the closeness he feels to God that fills his soul.

His unfailing advocacy for God and humankind leads to his crucifixion. Despite everything that may seem to the contrary, even at this time God never leaves his side. And a miracle occurs: the border separating life and death is removed. Having risen from the dead he inspires the living and gives courage to those who believe, he invites us to follow his example and for our closeness to God and our love for others to grow.

The Entry into Jerusalem

Pilgrims from all over Israel gather in Jerusalem to celebrate the feast of the Passover that recalls their deliverance from Egyptian slavery. Many people cheer Jesus, whose reputation for unusual deeds has preceded his arrival. They shout out 'Hosanna!' – originally a prayer of intercession in the Passover liturgy. 'O Lord, help us!' They place hope in God's messenger and direct their call for prayer at him. Has the moment now arrived when he is to liberate Israel from the Romans and (re)instate the glory of his people?

Jesus does not strive to fulfil any political expectations. The people sing: "Hosanna, the Son of God! He reigns supreme on the throne of David." However, he does not enter the city 'riding high on a great steed' like some powerful, battle-hungry warlord, but on a donkey, just as Zechariah had once told of the arrival of the Prince of Peace. He does not call on the people to rise up against the Romans but pleads for a different type of resisitance that stems from a new awareness of oneself and a new sense of self-confidence: "Blessed be those who spread peace, for they will be called the sons of God… You are the light of the world. Let your light shine before the people so that they may see your deeds and praise your Father in Heaven!" And he also demonstrates a different approach towards sinners as can be seen in the mercy he shows adulterers.

TABLEAU VIVANT

Paradise Lost   10 | 11

PASSION PLAY SCENES   13–16

The disciples brought the donkey and Jesus mounted it. The crowd that went before him and followed behind shouted out: "Blessed is he that cometh in the name of the Lord". Matthew 21:9 But when he saw the multitude "he opened his mouth, and taught them". Matthew 5:19 The Pharisees drew closer and said: "Master, we know that thou art true … Tell us therefore, What thinkest thou? Is it lawful to give tribute unto Caesar, or not? Jesus said, Why tempt ye me? Show me the tribute money. And he saith unto them, Whose is this image and superscription? They say unto him, Caesar's. Then saith he unto them, Render therefore unto Caesar the things which are Caesar's; and unto God the things that are God's". See Matthew 22:16–21 "And the scribes brought unto him a woman taken in adultery; and they say unto him, Master, this woman was taken in adultery, in the very act. Now Moses in the law commanded us, that such should be stoned: but what sayest thou? This they said, tempting him, that they might have to accuse him. But Jesus said unto them, He that is without sin among you, let him first cast a stone at her". See John 8:3–7

IN BETHANY

n **Bethany,** a village near Jerusalem on the eastern flanks of the Mount of Olives, friends and followers crowd around Jesus, brimming with joy. Jesus has come from the Mount of Olives and entered through the Gate of Mercy, as had been expected from the 'Lord's Anointed'. And is it not he who also brought about what had been prophesied? "Let the blind see again, the lame walk, lepers be cured, the deaf hear once more and the message of joy told to the humble!" The people receive him jubilantly, waving palm fronds frenetically, as they would for a king. Who is this man? And what gives him such authority? Peter answers by saying: "You are the Messiah." His declaration means: "Through him, God is close to us." Exactly this – namely passing on the message of God's closeness – is what Jesus demands of his friends, sending them out "like sheep among wolves".

This optimistic mood for the times ahead is utterly dashed as Mary Magdalene anoints Jesus' forehead and he surprises everyone when he explains the meaning of this gesture: "She has anointed my body for burial." He goes on to say that he will be "mocked, scourged and killed" in Jerusalem. Doubt and despair spread among the disciples. Together with several other relatives who have just arrived, Mary Magdalene tries to stop Jesus returning to the city. Only his mother acquiesces to her son's plans: "Off to Jerusalem! To the temple I once carried you to, to bring you to God! He gave you to me. Now he is asking for you to return."

Judas succinctly expresses the doubt felt by the disciples: "Your great deeds led us to believe that you would reinstate the Kingdom of Israel. Now you are talking about parting and dying and comfort us with mysterious words about the future which, for me, is too far away and still lies in darkness. I'm tiring of having to believe and hope."

Moses leads the Israelites through the Red Sea

As a tableau vivant, the scene in Bethany precedes the escape of the Israelites through the Red Sea. This introduces the elements of suspense – danger and salvation, death and life – that are so important to events in the Passion Play. The Israelites, guided by Moses, flee from the Egyptians into the sea and are witness to the seemingly impossible: unlike their persecutors, they enter a new life of freedom. And Jesus? Quite unexpectedly, he announces in Bethany that he will be killed. Like Moses, he too is following a path that, without faith in God, would appear to be without hope.

TABLEAU VIVANT

Moses leads the Israelites through the Red Sea 18 | 19

PASSION PLAY SCENES 20–24
Six days before the Feast of the Passover, Jesus arrived in Bethany where Lazarus was, who Jesus had restored to life. "Then took Mary a pound of ointment of spikenard, very costly, and anointed the feet of Jesus". John 12:3 "Jesus said unto them, The Son of man shall be betrayed into the hands of men: And they shall kill him … And they were exceeding sorry". Matthew 17:22–23 "Then Peter took him, and began to rebuke him, saying … Lord: this shall not be unto thee. But he turned, and said unto Peter, Get thee behind me, Satan: thou art an offence unto me: for thou savourest not the things that be of God, but those that be of men". Matthew 16:22–23 "While he yet talked to the people, behold, his mother and his brethren stood without, desiring to speak with him". Matthew 12:46

IN FRONT OF THE TEMPLE

Jesus arrives at the temple and proclaims the greatest words in the tradition of Israel among the chaos of activity: "Shema Yisrael! Hear, O Israel: the Lord our God, the Lord is one. And thou shalt love the Lord your God with all thine heart and with all thy soul and with all thy might. For there is no other commandment greater than this" (see Deuteronomy 6). The focus he places is on God. He throws the stall-holders selling animals to be sacrificed and the money-lenders who have taken over the temple out of the building.

The ruling bodies of Jerusalem see this as an attack on their authority and question the legitimization of Jesus' actions – and Jesus in turn questions theirs: "The scribes and the Pharisees sit in Moses' seat: / All therefore whatsoever they bid you observe, that observe and do; but do not ye after their works: for they say, and do not" (Matthew 23:2–3). In a moment of silence, the people join in common prayer, saying: "Shema yisrael adonai eloheinu adonai echad."

After Jesus leaves, several urge Caiaphas, the high priest, to put a stop to what this 'heretic' is doing. He is put under considerably greater pressure when Pontius Pilate, the powerful Equestrian procurator of the Roman province of Judaea, appears and warns him: "Should it come to disunion in the country and a revolt against Rome, I shall descend upon you with my army and bring ruin and destruction upon you, your country and your people." On top of this he threatens Caiaphas personally, who to a certain extent thanked the Roman his career in the first place: "Should peace not return to the city, I shall take back everything I have given you."

During the meeting of the High Council – many of whom are members of the aristrocratic Sadduccees – that follows, the measures to be taken against Jesus and the possibility of his imprisonment are discussed. When Judas appears, unsettled and agitated as to his belief in Jesus, Caiaphas manages to deceive him: "It is necessary for me to speak to him, for this and only for this reason I shall seek him out." Judas promises to show him where Jesus can be found in the evening.

The Ten Commandments and the Dance around the Golden Calf

Feeling the mounting resistance he is facing, Jesus experiences the same fate as many prophets. They are 'signs which will be contradicted'. They demand a decision – in favour or against the message they bring. This tableau vivant is just such an example: when Moses comes down from Mount Sinai with God's message and sees the people dancing around the golden calf, he demands they decide whether to serve God or the idol of their own power.

TABLEAU VIVANT

The Ten Commandments and the Dance around the Golden Calf **26 | 27**

PASSION PLAY SCENES **28–34**

"And Jesus went into the temple of God, and cast out all them that sold and bought in the temple, and overthrew the tables … And said unto them, It is written, My house shall be called a house of prayer, but ye have made it a den of thieves". Matthew 21:12–13; see Isaiah 56:7 And when the Sadducees approached him, Jesus said to them: "Hear, O Israel; The Lord our God is one Lord: And thou shalt love the Lord thy God with all thy heart, and with all thy soul, and with all thy mind, and with all thy strength". Mark 12:29–30 And he said: "Think not that I am come to destroy the law, or the prophets: I am not come to destroy, but to fulfil". Matthew 5:17 The high priests called a meeting of the Supreme Council and asked: "What shall we do?" This happened when "Pontius Pilate was governor of Judaea and Caiaphas the high priest". see Luke 3:1–2 "And Judas Iscariot, one of the twelve, went unto the chief priests, to betray him unto them". Mark 14:10

THE LAST SUPPER

T he evening of the Passover approaches. The whole of Israel celebrates this feast in the hope that God will once again come to save them – perhaps in the days to come – just as he had liberated his people in the past from the hands of the Egyptians. Jesus' disciples, however, are bewildered, disappointed and despondent after what he said in Bethany. They despair: "We had hoped for light, but instead darkness has fallen upon us." Have Jesus' commitment and the efforts of the disciples on his behalf – for whose sake they have neglected everything else – been unsuccessful? Jesus does not try to comfort them. In view of this danger in particular Jesus asks for compassion towards the needy, the hungry and the imprisoned. To exemplify what he means, he does something that is usually a servant's job when guests enter a house: he washes their feet.

During the course of the ritual Passover ceremony when it is time to break the bread and bless the wine, Jesus gives these ancient gestures an unexpected turn. Looking ahead to his imminent death, he offers himself, his own life, in the bread and wine, in order to become one with his friends in such a way that nothing, not even his death, can separate them. But a shadow is also cast upon this meal. "As soon as Judas had taken the bread, he went out. And it was night" (John 13:30).

The Feast of Passover before the Exodus from Egypt

The tableau before the Last Supper depicts the dramatic moment during the meal that the Israelites celebrated the night before their exodus from Egypt. Just at the moment when they expect to be rescued, while feeling the threat of Egypt's supremacy, a lamb is sacrificed. An angel passes by to protect the families whose doors have been marked with the blood of the lamb. The experience of the saviour God of Israel is also borne by Jesus in this hour. The tableau is shocking insofar as the first-born children of Egypt who have been killed, can also be seen. The path of life for the Israelites together with their god is in stark contrast to the path of death. But is it always the case that the salvation of one person means that another must perish?

ON THE MOUNT OF OLIVES

After the feast of the Passover, Jesus and his disciples go to the Mount of Olives. The irrevocable decision is reached among the olive trees of Gethsemane. Jesus knows what is awaiting him. In his mind he experiences in advance his death at Golgotha, as is written in the Epistle to the Hebrews: "During the days of Jesus' life on earth, he offered up prayers and petitions with loud cries and tears to the one who could save him from death…" (Hebrews 5:7).

As Mark writes, Jesus was "deeply distressed and troubled" and, in prayer, utters his powerful lamentation using the words of Psalm 42: "As the deer pants for streams of water / so my soul pants for you, O God / …My tears have been my food day and night / while men say to me all day long / 'Where is your God?' / …My soul is downcast within me / …all your waves and breakers / have swept over me."

Jesus, who taught his disciples the pledge of the Lord's Prayer – "Thy will be done", now himself beseeches: "If it is possible, may this cup be taken from me" (Matthew 26:39). Although he adds: "Yet not as I will, but as you will", it is obvious that this message brings him to the very limits of what can be endured.

An angel appears and consoles him: "Take upon yourself the ills of mankind. Let yourself be pierced by their crimes, crushed by their sins. Heal them through your wounds. I make you a light for the people, so that my salvation reaches even to the ends of the earth" (see Isaiah 53).

God calls Moses from the Burning Bush

An analogy to the Mount of Olives scene is when Moses hears the voice of God from the burning thorn bush commanding him to go to the Pharaoh and demand that he set Israel free. Moses is afraid that this is more than he is capable of doing. He resists the task until he receives the pledge that God will be with him: "Yahwe" – meaning "I am he who will abide by you" – at which time God reveals who is in front of him.

THE INTERROGATION BEFORE ANNAS AND THE SUPREME COUNCIL

Taken prisoner, led away and summoned for questioning – events follow in quick succession. And no time passes before Jesus is interrogated by Annas, the 'éminence grise'. Asked about 'his disciples and his teaching', he refuses to answer directly. "I have always taught in synagogues and at the temple and said nothing in secret. Why are you questioning me?" Annas' servant hits Jesus in the face for this reply – the first time that his physical integrity is infringed. Whenever those in power feel their authority being questioned, the threat of violence is very real. This has been experienced by countless people serving God, from Isaiah to the martyrs of the Third Reich, and some – such as Jeanne d'Arc, Juan de la Cruz and others – from Christian authorities too. Caiaphas calls a secret meeting at night to interrogate Jesus, to which – contrary to Jewish prohibitions – only council members are invited who are loyal to him. However, supporters and followers of Jesus also attend. A heated discussion takes place about key questions. Firstly, whether Jesus has been acting in the name of the God of Israel and his laws; secondly, if he is allowed to call himself the 'Son of God' or even the Messiah. Caiaphas feels that a military attack against the Roman rulers is to be feared. "Take pity on your country, the temple, your womenfolk and children, and do not put everything at stake for the sake of one single Galilean." Since Jesus' admission to being the Messiah, from the point of view of traditionalists, automatically introduces leadership claims and as such is a challenge to Rome, Caiaphas decides to pass the case over to Pontius Pilate.

The Prophet Daniel in the Lions' Den

This tableau depicting the prophet Daniel precedes the series of unjust accusations. Representatives of the official Babylonian state religion accuse Daniel of continuing to pray to the God of Israel and he is thrown into the lions' den. Like Daniel, Jesus holds firm to his faith. In ignominy and ignobility God abides by him as he did the prophet.

TABLEAU VIVANT

The Prophet Daniel in the Lions' Den   56 | 57

PASSION PLAY SCENES   59–62

"Then the band and the captain and officers of the Jews took Jesus, and bound him, And led him away to Annas first; for he was father in law to Caiaphas, which was the high priest that same year". John 18:12–13 And then they "led him away to Caiaphas the high priest, where the scribes and the elders were assembled. They sought false witness against Jesus, to put him to death; yea, though many false witnesses came, yet found they none. And the high priest said unto him, I adjure thee by the living God, that thou tell us whether thou be the Christ, the Son of God. Jesus saith unto him, Thou hast said. Then the high priest rent his clothes, saying, He hath spoken blasphemy; behold, now ye have heard his blasphemy. What think ye? They answered and said, He is guilty of death". See Matthew 26:57–66

THE MOCKERY OF JESUS – PETER'S BETRAYAL AND REMORSE

After being interrogated, Jesus becomes the object of his guards' mocking games. As trials against war criminals have shown, a certain tendency to ruthless games and rituals obviously evolves among certain groups of people. Perhaps the soldiers are also secretly afraid of Jesus, since he is said to have prophetic gifts and unusual powers. In any case, they mock him and try to poke fun at him. Jesus increasingly experiences how humans can be humiliated; he suffers from a loss of respect and dignity.

Unlike Jesus, Peter tries to evade suffering – and finds suffering of a different kind instead. He, the fisherman from the Sea of Galilee, who emerges as a particularly bold, tough disciple and who obviously has such a strong character that Jesus calls him the 'rock', breaks down. When he is identified as one of Jesus' disciples in the courtyard outside Annas' house, he is filled with fear and swears: "I do not know this man." No sooner has he betrayed Jesus, he himself experiences the humiliation of one who has betrayed another. Perhaps it is from looking into Jesus' eyes that he gains the courage to repent and, despite this breach of trust, to return to the fold.

Job in Misery

The tableau vivant that precedes this scene shows Job, the archetype of the suffering human being. The Chorus comments: "Yet he bears his afflictions patiently. / Beset on all sides by scorn and derision / he trusts, hoping, in his God. / No word of complaint issues from him." There is a time to speak and a time to hold ones tongue. Jesus, however, questions the soldier who hit out at him, in the presence of Annas: "If I have spoken evil, bear witness of the evil: but if well, why smitest thou me?" (John 18:23). While on earth Jesus intervened in many conflicts and spoke out for the weak and humiliated. Now he leaves it to his Father to bring about justice, not making any accusations or talking of revenge or violence, as every act of revenge only leads to an endless chain of new acts of violence.

TABLEAU VIVANT

Job in Misery   64 | 65

PASSION PLAY SCENES   66–69

"And the men that held Jesus mocked him, and smote him. And when they had blindfolded him, they [...] asked him, saying, Prophesy, who is it that smote thee? And many other things blasphemously spake they against him". Luke 22:63–65 "Now Peter sat without in the palace: and a damsel came unto him, saying, Thou also wast with Jesus of Galilee. But he denied before them all, saying, I know not what thou sayest. And when he was gone out into the porch, another maid saw him, and said unto them that were there, This fellow was also with Jesus of Nazareth. And again he denied with an oath, I do not know the man. And after a while came unto him they that stood by, and said to Peter, Surely thou also art one of them; for thy speech bewrayeth thee. Then began he to curse and to swear, saying, I know not the man. And immediately the cock crew. And Peter remembered the word of Jesus, which said unto him, Before the cock crow, thou shalt deny me thrice. And he went out, and wept bitterly". Matthew 26:69–75

JUDAS' DESPAIR

Smite the shepherd, and the sheep shall be scattered" (Zechariah 13:7; see also Matthew 26:31). With this quotation from the Book of Zechariah Jesus points to exactly what happens to the disciples after his arrest. It is not merely a pupil/teacher relationship that is torn apart. The truth that a person finds his or her real identity in a personal relationship, when 'you' becomes 'I', is certainly the case in the relationship between those who answered his call and Jesus himself. One can only suppose how he enriched and inspired their lives, awakening the spiritual within them and, conversely, what the loss of his being at their side must have meant to them. When this bond was torn, the threads of their own existences were left hanging in a void. (The importance of this relationship can also be seen in how, later on, the disciples did everything possible – right up to martyrdom – after the Resurrection to uphold this relationship.)

This also applies to the disciple Judas Iscariot. Jesus also selected him, spoke to him as a brother, a friend; he let him partake of the bread and washed his feet. Why Judas revealed where Jesus could be found remains a mystery – it certainly was not purely for material gain. According to St. Mark and St. Luke he did not demand any payment for his services; it was the high priests who offered it to him. He is horrified when, in front of Annas, he finally realises that Jesus could be killed. Guilt weighs heavily on his shoulders. After his attempt at saving Jesus fails, he gives back the money and commits suicide. Unlike in Peter's case, Judas is not borne by his faith in Jesus and does not find his way back to the fold.

Cain's Despair

Judas' despair is the mirror image of Cain's. His example tells us that whenever someone is culpable of another's death, this directly affects the relationship of the guilty party to God, as the God of Israel is not only the Creator but also the protector of life, to whom all are accountable. Although Judas does not have anything directly to do with Jesus' death, he nevertheless feels guilty. Instead of turning back, as Peter does, he despairs, like Cain. He passes judgment on himself and forestalls God's mercy, for in his eyes the possibility always remains of becoming a different person.

TABLEAU VIVANT

Cain's Despair   70 | 71

PASSION PLAY SCENES   73–74

"Then Judas, which had betrayed him, when he saw that he was condemned, repented himself, and brought again the thirty pieces of silver to the chief priests and elders, Saying, I have sinned in that I have betrayed the innocent blood. And they said, What is that to us? see thou to that. And he cast down the pieces of silver in the temple, and departed, and went and hanged himself".   Matthew 27:3–5

BEFORE PONTIUS PILATE AND HEROD

Jesus is handed over to Pontius Pilate, the Roman governor of Judea. "Venality, violence, unlawful appropriation of property, continued executions without legal proceedings, incessant and unbearable cruelty" – these are just some of the accusations held against him by his contemporary Philo. Although Luke reports that Pontius Pilate had Galilean pilgrims butchered in the temple (Luke 13:1), the gospels are otherwise kind to the image of this man of power who looks to his own advantage without consideration for others. This also applies to the relationship with Caiaphas whom he treats as a protégé on the one hand and yet tyrannises him on the other. His hesitancy in convicting Jesus is not out of sympathy, but because he does not want to give Caiaphas the necessary authority to act – and out of diplomatic caution. His reputation in Rome has already been damaged and he will later be removed from office due to his excessive zeal. In addition, he miscalculates, hoping that if he offers Jesus as an alternative to Barabbas within the terms of the Passover amnesty, he will be able to keep the latter in prison, politically the more dangerous, and increase his popularity among the people. The fact that he orders Jesus to be flogged, is without any legal foundation.

In Jesus, Pontius Pilate is faced by his absolute opposite. He represents a new dimension in human relationships – a realm in which God's benevolence towards humankind will be fulfilled. Pontius Pilate, however, dismisses Jesus' claim with a shrug of his shoulders saying: "What is truth?"

Jesus' appearance before Herod Antipas is a bizarre interlude. Politically of little weight – he is not a king but a tetrarch of a small region under Roman rule – and barely recognised by the people because of his non-Jewish decent, Herod lives a life of dissipation devoted to his passion for building and love of magnificence. Having had John the Baptist, the preacher of repentance, put to death, he suspects that Jesus is John returned from the dead. Once this fear is put to rest, he asks Jesus to perform some sensational miracle as a sign. Not unlike some people of our own age, he is able only to comprehend the world as a spectacle, as a consumer item.

Moses is Cast out by the Pharaoh

The tableau before this encounter between Jesus and Pontius Pilate is the scene in which Moses challenges Egypt's ruler: "Thus saith the Lord God of Israel, Let my people go", and the Pharaoh replies: "Who is the Lord, that I should obey his voice to let Israel go? I know not the Lord" (Exodus 5:1–2). In both cases, a power system blocks out reality that calls its own standards into question – as not infrequently the case in the 20th century.

"When the morning was come, [...] they had bound him, they led him away, and delivered him to Pontius Pilate the governor. / Then said Pilate unto him, Hearest thou not how many things they witness against thee?" Matthew 27:1–2, 13 "And as soon as he knew that he belonged unto Herod's jurisdiction, he sent him to Herod, who himself also was at Jerusalem at that time. And when Herod saw Jesus, he was exceeding glad: for he was desirous to see him of a long season, because he had heard many things of him; and he hoped to have seen some miracle done by him. Then he questioned with him in many words; but he answered him nothing. [...] And Herod with his men of war set him at nought, and mocked him, and arrayed him in a gorgeous robe, and sent him again to Pilate". Luke 23:7–11 "And Jesus stood before the governor: and the governor asked him, saying, Art thou the King of the Jews? And Jesus said unto him, Thou sayest". Matthew 27:11 "Then the soldiers of the governor took Jesus into the common hall, and gathered unto him the whole band of soldiers. And they stripped him, and put on him a scarlet robe. And when they had platted a crown of thorns, they put it upon his head, and a reed in his right hand: and they bowed the knee before him, and mocked him, saying, Hail, King of the Jews! And they spit upon him, and took the reed, and smote him on the head". Matthew 27:27–30

PONTIUS PILATE CONDEMNS JESUS TO DEATH

Without first determining Jesus' guilt according to standard legal proceedings, in other words without any right to detain him at all, Pontius Pilate uses Jesus as the object of a tactical manoeuvre, an amnesty: Jesus of Nazareth or the insurgent Barabbas – the ordinary people should decide. Pontius Pilate expects the choice to fall in favour of Jesus – in his opinion the less politically significant. He counts on the overwhelming sympathy felt for Jesus and hopes, by pardoning him, to be seen in a favourable light by the people and be able to keep Barabbas behind bars.

"But the chief priests moved the people, that he should rather release Barabbas unto them" (Mark 15:11) – despite the opposition shown by Jesus' followers. The group of leaders under Caiaphas calls its supporters, its claqueurs, to where court is being held. The strategy followed by the cynical, much-hated procurator and the demagogic zeal of Jesus' opponents contribute to the mood tipping in favour of Barabbas. It soons seems as if it has nothing to do with Jesus at all, but is merely a question of the people getting their own back on Pontius Pilate, the occupier.

All legal instances fail, both the state-appointed judge who grotesquely washes his hands 'in innocence', as well as the crowd. The 'voice of the people – the voice of God'; who can still believe in it? Just as before the Peoples' Court in Nazi Germany, all hopes for humanity and justice are dashed. The swirl of violence and counter-violence spins ever more quickly until, finally, someone is put to death. And one cannot help but feel astonished at the blindness of those who witnessed the year 1934 and did not recognise this scene as a mirror of their own circumstances.

Joseph is Celebrated as the Saviour of Egypt

This moment in which Jesus becomes ever less recognisable as the bringer of salvation to the people, is preceded by a tableau of Joseph in Egypt as the epitome of a celebrated, radiant man of God and a saviour. The tableau asks the question: can God's voice be present in somebody who remains silent? Can we expect help from somebody who was not even able to help himself?

TABLEAU VIVANT

Joseph is Celebrated as the Saviour of Egypt 88 | 89

PASSION PLAY SCENES 91–95

"Now at that feast the governor was wont to release unto the people a prisoner, whom they would. And they had then a notable prisoner, called Barabbas. The chief priests and elders persuaded the multitude that they should ask Barabbas. And when they had gathered Pilate said unto them, Whether of the twain will ye that I release unto you? They said, Barabbas. Pilate saith unto them, What shall I do then with Jesus which is called Christ? They all say unto him, Let him be crucified. When Pilate saw that that rather a tumult was made, he took water, and washed his hands. And delivered Jesus to be crucified".
See Matthew 27:15–26

ON THE WAY OF THE CROSS

John brings Mary the news that Jesus has been flogged. The torture is the preliminary stage to crucifixion – as all those around him are well aware. "The hour has come that he foresaw."

After being sentenced by Pontius Pilate, a cross is laid on Jesus' shoulders, as those condemned to death had to carry it themselves to the place of execution. Outside the city walls, expelled from the community.

Physical aspects come to the fore: the heat, the shouting, the soldiers' orders, the screams of pain. "All who saw him, mocked him, opened their mouths wide and shouted. No longer a human, ridiculed by the masses, despised by the people" (see Psalm 22). Jesus stumbles and is pulled back onto his feet. The resurgent noise, people staring at him in surprise or full of curiosity. And suddenly among them is the face of his mother. She recalls Simeon's prophecy: "[There shall be] a sign which shall be spoken against; …a sword shall pierce through thy own soul also" (Luke 2:34–35).

And once again the henchman's blows. Once again he falls to the ground. The soldiers make a nearby stranger carry the cross for him. Women draw in closer, lamenting, weeping for him. He prophesies: "…Weep not for me, but weep for yourselves, and for your children. For, behold, the days are coming, …Then shall they begin to say to the mountains, Fall on us; and to the hills, Cover us. For if they do these things in a green tree, what shall be done in the dry?" (Luke 23:28–31).

Isaac carries Wood up Mount Moriah

Isaac is a paradigm for Jesus bearing the cross. His father, Abraham, believed he had to sacrifice his beloved son on Mount Moriah, as commanded by his inscrutable god. Isaac himself carried the wood for the fire on which his son was to be burnt up the mountain. The story of this absolute trust in God ends with God revealing that what matters to him is not human sacrifce but a heart that is prepared to give itself completely to him. As in the case of Jesus.

TABLEAU VIVANT

Isaac carries Wood up Mount Moriah   96 | 97

PASSION PLAY SCENES   99–104

"And he bearing his cross went forth into a place called the place of a skull, which is called in the Hebrew Golgotha". John 19:17 "And many women were there beholding afar off, which followed Jesus from Galilee, ministering unto him: Among which was Mary Magdalene, and Mary the mother of James and Joses, and the mother of Zebedees children". Matthew 27:55–56 "And as they came out, they found a man of Cyrene, Simon by name: him they compelled to bear his cross". Matthew 27:32 "And there followed him a great company of people, and of women, which also bewailed and lamented him. But Jesus turning unto them said, Daughters of Jerusalem, weep not for me, but weep for yourselves, and for your children". Luke 23:27–28

THE CRURIFIXION

THE CRUCIFIXION

They reach Golgotha, a rocky hill just outside the city: the band of soldiers, Jesus' opponents, relatives and followers, women espcially and those condemned to death. Stripped of their clothes, they are nailed to the crosses which are then raised into position. Above Jesus' head is a notice with the charge against him: 'Jesus of Nazareth, King of the Jews' – the Romans understand the Jewish concept of the Messiah, the Lord's Annointed, only as a claim to royal powers. The notice gives rise to doubts, mockery and controversy that has continued to this day: how can it be a king on the cross?

An agonising death begins. The soldiers divide up Jesus' belongings. Mary and John stand under the cross. Jesus draws them together, founding a community which countless others will later join.

"My God, my God, why hast thou foresaken me?" (see Psalms 22) Jesus cries out the opening words of the psalm that alternates between despair and hope. "But I am a worm, and no man; a reproach of men … / … Praise the Lord! … For he hath not despised nor abhorred the affliction of the afflicted; neither hath he hid his face from him." Jesus feels deserted – he does not feel his Father's hands into which he commits his spirit. Finally, Jesus "gave up the ghost" (Mark 15:37).

To ensure he is dead, an officer pierces his side with a spear "and forthwith came there out blood and water" (John 19:34). "Thus Jesus' heart remains open through all erternity, in order to refresh with the mysterious living source that gushes forth from him all those who labour and are heavy laden" (Urs von Balthasar). He is taken down from the cross and laid to rest in a nearby tomb.

And then? Normally death marks a definitive end to life. Everything else goes against the laws of nature. And then Mary Magdalene, the Twelve, Paul and other disciples make an uplifting discovery: Jesus of Nazareth has risen again! "O death, where is thy sting? O grave, where is they victory?" (1st Corinthians 15:55).

"Where they crucified him, and two other with him, on either side one, and Jesus in the midst". John 19:18
"Now there stood by the cross of Jesus his mother, and his mother's sister, and Mary Magdalene. When Jesus therefore saw his mother, and the disciple standing by, whom he loved, he saith unto his mother, Woman, behold thy son! Then saith he to the disciple, Behold thy mother! And from that hour that disciple took her unto his own home". John 19:25–27
"And about the ninth hour Jesus cried with a loud voice, saying, Eli,Eli, lama sabachtani? that is to say, My God, my God, why hast thou forsaken me? / Jesus, when he had cried again with a loud voice, yielded up the ghost". Matthew 27:46, 50

"When the even was come, there came a rich man of Arimathaea, named Joseph. / And when Joseph had taken the body, he wrapped it in a clean linen cloth, And laid it in his own new tomb, which he had hewn out in the rock: and he rolled a great stone to the door of the sepulchre, and departed". Matthew 27:57, 59–60

"And when the sabbath was past, Mary Magdalene, and Mary the mother of James, and Salome, had bought sweet spices, that they might come and anoint him. / And entering into the sepulchre, they saw a young man sitting on the right side […] and they were affrighted. And he saith unto them, Be not affrighted: Ye seek Jesus of Nazareth, which was crucified: he is risen; he is not here". Mark 16:1, 5–6

"And, lo, I am with you alway, even unto the end of the world". Matthew 28:20

Looking upon the Fiery Serpent

The tableau vivant focuses on the relationship to the cross. Just as the Israelites, wounded by snake bites, were healed by looking upon the 'fiery serpent' (Numbers 21:8) that Moses set upon a pole – so whoever gazes at Jesus on the cross gains strength to live. "And as Moses lifted up the serpent in the wilderness, even so must the Son of man be lifted up / That whosoever believeth in him should not perish, but have eternal life" (John 3 14:15).

ACTORS, ACTRESSES AND SOLOISTS

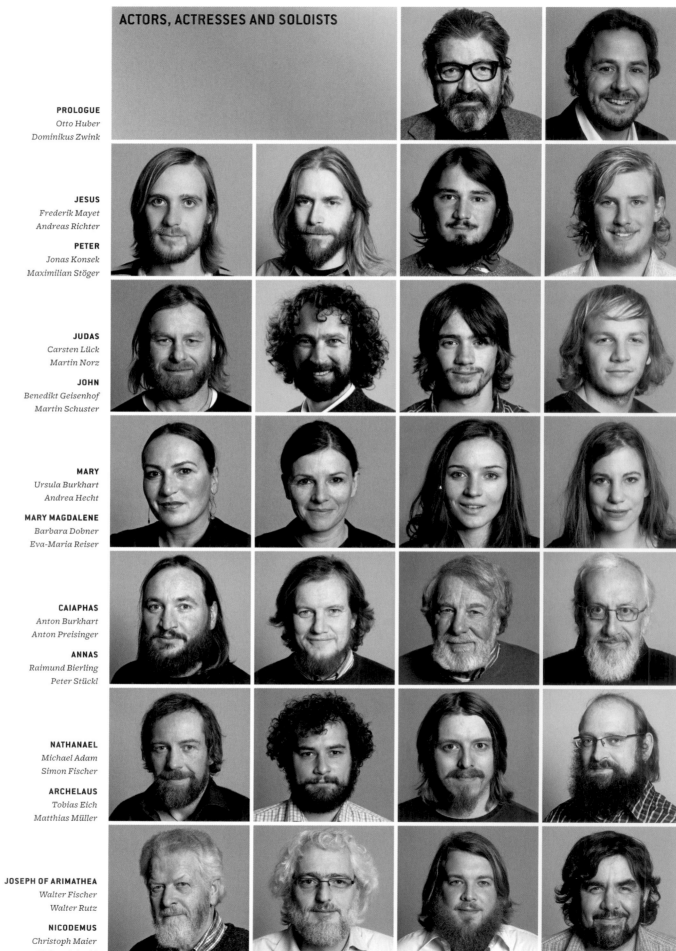

PROLOGUE
Otto Huber
Dominikus Zwink

JESUS
Frederik Mayet
Andreas Richter

PETER
Jonas Konsek
Maximilian Stöger

JUDAS
Carsten Lück
Martin Norz

JOHN
Benedikt Geisenhof
Martin Schuster

MARY
Ursula Burkhart
Andrea Hecht

MARY MAGDALENE
Barbara Dobner
Eva-Maria Reiser

CAIAPHAS
Anton Burkhart
Anton Preisinger

ANNAS
Raimund Bierling
Peter Stückl

NATHANAEL
Michael Adam
Simon Fischer

ARCHELAUS
Tobias Eich
Matthias Müller

JOSEPH OF ARIMATHEA
Walter Fischer
Walter Rutz

NICODEMUS
Christoph Maier
Hubert Schmid

GAMALIEL
Johannes Müller
Stephan Reindl

EZEKIEL
Martin Güntner
Tobias Jablonka

PONTIUS PILATE
Christian Bierling
Stephan Burkhart

HEROD
Raimund Fussy
Markus Köpf

LONGINUS
Johann Feldmeier
Ferdinand Meiler

SIMON OF BETHANY
Karl Führler
Anton Zwink

VERONICA
Elisabeth Aurhammer
Dominika Killer

ANGEL
Sebastian Dörfler
Maximilian Laubert

SOPRANO
Maria Buchwieser
Katharina Osterhammer
Gabriele Weinfurter-Zwink

ALTO
Caroline Fischer-Zwink

ALTO
Claudia Köpf
Antonie Schauer

TENOR
Paul Fellner
Korbinian Heinzeller

TENOR
Michael Pfaffenzeller

BASSO
Heinrich Buchwieser
Bernhard Spingler
Josef Zwink

Chronology

OF THE OBERAMMERGAU PASSION PLAY

1633 In the beginning was the vow. After the Thirty Years War, the Black Death reachd Oberammergau in 1632. By October of the following year 80 deaths had been recorded. At that time it was reported how "…at this time of suffering, the village councils of the Six and the Twelve met and vowed to perform the Passion Play every ten years." Since it was the Parish Elders who took the vow, the Passion Play has remained the responsibility of the local council ever since.

1634 1st Passion Play. At Whitsun, "the play of the suffering, death, and resurrection of our Lord Jesus Christ" is reenacted by 60 to 70 actors next to the church, among the recently dug graves of victims of the Black Death.

1644, 1654, 1664 2nd/3rd/4th Passion Plays. The schoolmaster, Georg Kaiser, completes a script in 1662 for the 4th Passion Play, the oldest text to have survived to this day. His note that the text has been 'revised again', indicates that a similar text had been used in 1634, 1644 and 1654. The 4,902 verses are a combination of two versions of the passion play of an earlier date. The first is from the latter half of the 15th century, that in turn is based on one once performed in Tyrol. The second is the *Tragedi Passion* by Sebastian Wild, Master Singer of Augsburg, that was printed in 1566 and had been inspired by reformist principles. From the very outset, an ecumenical text is used.

1674, 1680 5th/6th Passion Plays. Expanded to include scenes from the Weilheim Passion (1600, 1615) by the parish priest Johannes Älbl. Date moved to the first year of every decade.

1690, 1700, 1710 7th/8th/9th Passion Plays. The earliest surviving accounts sheets mention 'expenses for the Passion Play': 45 florins, 45 kreuzers. 1700: expenditure for 'the trumpeters from Ettal' and for costumes borrowed from Rottenbuch Monastery.

1720 10th Passion Play. Text revised by the Benedictine monk Karl Bader of Ettal (1662–1731).

1730 11th Passion Play. Text adapted by the Augustinian canon Anselm Manhardt (1680–1752) of Rottenbuch, who introduces Satan and the allegorical figures of Hell – Jealousy, Avarice, Sin and Death – as enemies of Jesus. Two performances. Total debt: 84 florins.

1740 12th Passion Play. Text revised by Clemens Prasser (1703–1770), vicar of Oberammergau and later provost of Rottenbuch. Probably performed twice.

1750 13th Passion Play. Responding to criticism voiced in the Age of Reason that the most sacred story of Christianity had no place on a stage, the villagers in Oberammergau seek a new form of presentation. An eloquent and pious scriptwriter is found in the person of the Benedictine monk Ferdinand Rosner (1709–1778) of Ettal, who pulls all the registers of the sacred Baroque theater in the 8,457 verses of his Passio nova. He introduces a meditative element. The performance is divided by seven musically accompanied 'Observations' comprising three tableaux vivants in each instance. While remaining complete static, the actors introduce a pictorial composition from the parables of Jesus Christ or scenes from the history of Israel. The use of analogies clearly shows what is happening to Jesus. The text gains in popularity in Bavaria and the Oberammergau Passion Play becomes a model for performances in other places.

1760 14th Passion Play. Two performances attended by 14,000 spectators.

1770 All Passion Plays are banned in Bavaria. A special appeal by Oberammergau is rejected in spite of intensive efforts. The deficit from lost revenue: 274 florins.

1780 15th Passion Play. Oberammergau is granted special permission. The revised script by the Benedictine monk Magnus Knipfelberger (1747–1825) of Ettal, avoids

 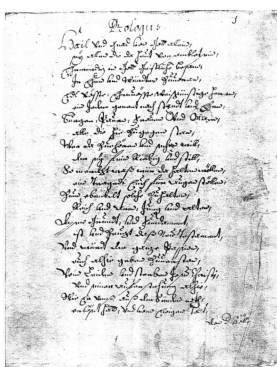 

any mention of the theme of the Passion in the title by calling it *The Old and New Testaments*.

1790 16th Passion Play. Permission for five performances is granted (11,000 spectators). The Play is first mentioned in a newspaper and tickets issued for the first time. A profit of 600 florins is made.

1800 17th Passion Play. Renewed permission. The Napoleonic Wars result in the number of spectators dropping to c. 3,000. The village council contributes 205 florins.

1801 18th Passion Play. In order to reduce the debt incurred by the wars, special permission is given to hold four performances.

1810 The minister Count Maximilian Montgelas, a critic of the Church, revokes the permission granted to Oberammergau. There are no performances.

1811 19th Passion Play. Permission is granted to hold performances once again, after a new text reflecting the aesthetics and theology of the times has been submitted for approval. In his text, Othmar Weis (1769–1843), the last monk of Ettal following secularisation, concentrates on the gospels, eliminates legendary, mythological and allegorical elements, focuses on Realism, and adopts prose rather than verse and a secular rather than biblical narrative style. He incorporates contemporary issues, introduces moralising interpretations – on social justice, for instance – and draws attention to the pivotal notion of atonement. Rochus Dedler (1779–1822), a teacher and musician born in Oberammergau, composes the music for the Play, especially that used for the tableaux vivants which, even today, is still characteristic of the Play.

1815 20th Passion Play. Special performances are held to give thanks for the end of the Napoleonic Wars. New texts are added and an extensive revision of the existing one made by Weis, and of the music by Dedler (up until 1820). Expansion of the crowd scenes, such as the 'Entry

into Jerusalem'. A new theatre is designed in the Empire Style by Father Johann Nikolaus Unhoch (1762–1832), with a wide proscenium and a changeable central stage section, flanked by two-storeyed buildings with 'alleyways' and arcades leading off to the sides.

1820 21st Passion Play. Oldest eye-witness account by the royal planning officer Anton Baumgartner.

1830 22nd Passion Play. King Ludwig I refuses permission for the Play to be performed in the graveyard. The stage is erected on the north-west edge of the village. 5,000 spectators can be accommodated. Only 13,000 visitors attend the dress rehearsal and 10 performances.

1840 23rd Passion Play. 35,000 people attend. The increase in spectators is partly due to enthusiastic accounts in newspapers seen from a Romantic point of view by visitors to the Passion Plays in 1820 and 1830.

1850 24th Passion Play. The parish priest, Joseph Alois Daisenberger (1799–1883), directs the Play. In the spirit of Johann Michael Sailer, the learned theologian, historian and man of letters actively seeks to educate the people. He also publishes *The History of the Village of Oberammergau* and a number of historical works. 464 actors perform in front of some 45,000 spectators.

1860 25th Passion Play. Daisenberger revises the text at the government's request, taking account of the criticism made in 1850. He aims at timelessness instead of the updating preferred by Weis, at idealisation instead of Realism and at the psychological element instead of the political. Judas, for example, is no longer presented as the generally despised greedy devil, but as a doubter, full of worry and fear of being excluded from the heavenly realm. Daisenberger's use of symbols such as light and darkness corresponds to his preference for the Gospel of St. John. At the same time, he attempts to add popularity by (re-)introducing legends (Veronica, Ahasuerus) and

In the oldest surviving records in Oberammergau an entry for the period from September 1632 until October 1633 lists the names of eighty plague victims.

The prologue in the earliest existing manuscript of the text from 1662, with Protestant introduction: "Salvation and mercy from God alone…"

The Benedictine monk, Father Ferdinand Rosner (1709–1778) of Ettal, professor of rhetoric at the Ettal Knights' Academy, and author of the Passio nova *of 1750, entitled 'Wretched Suffering, Victorious Death and Glorious Resurrection of the Son of God made Man.'*

The Benedictine monk, Father Othmar Weis (1769–1843) of Ettal who, in his texts on the Passion, reacted to changes in the theatre and to the theology of his time, and contributed to the survival of this genre in the 19th century.

Rochus Dedler (1779–1822), a teacher and composer born in Oberammergau, wrote the music to accompany Othmar Weis's text for the Passion Plays in 1811, 1815 and 1820. Since no authentic portrait of Dedler exists, the artist M. Z. Diemer painted this imaginary portrait in 1920, based on contemporary descriptions.

The stage set designed by Johann Nikolaus Unhoch (1762–1832) for the Passion Play in 1815, which disbanded with elements of the Rococo and Classicism.

incidents on the Way of the Cross (Jesus meeting Mary), and by using emotional, vivid language and simple symbolism (the Cross as the Tree of Life).

Some 10,000 spectators, including King Maximillian II, attend a total of 21 performances.

1870 26th Passion Play. Daisenberger writes prologues to the tableaux vivants in the style of the German classical age using classical ode metres and blank verse for the texts. However, with the exception of the prologue, his proposal is not accepted by the village.

1871 26th Passion Play (continued after being interrupted by the war with France). "May the Play, this inheritance of a Germany of yore, witness our brethren from the north and the south united in love as citizens of a reborne Germany" – such was the announcement for the Oberammergau Passion Play in the periodical 'Germania.' Many of the estimated 40,000 visitors come from

the United States and England (including Crown Prince Edward), Richard Wagner, members of the aristocracy, King Ludwig II – who donates a monumental sculpture of the cruxifixion – and the court photographer Joseph Albert who documents the performance.

1880 27th Passion Play. As in Wagner's Festival Hall in Bayreuth the orchestra disppears from view into a pit. The boxes at the back are roofed over and a gallery added around the auditorium as standing room. Elaborate new scenery and new costumes are made – the latter in cooperation with the Royal Court Theatre in Munich. The extension of the railway to Murnau makes travelling that much easier and the London-based travel agency, Thomas Cook, introduces revolutionary forms of organised tourism. 100,000 spectators.

1890 28th Passion Play. The stage is rebuilt by the internationally renowned theatre technician Carl Lauten-

The advisor on spiritual matters and reformer of the Passion Play: Joseph Alois Daisenberger (1799–1883), who also directed the play from 1850 to 1870, photographed here in the summer of 1871 by Steigenberger and Johannes, Weilheim.

schläger in the neo-Renaissance style, incorporating state-of-the-art technology. By moving Anna's and Pilate's houses to either side of the stage, a new area is created to accommodate crowd scenes. A glazed roof over the central section permits natural light to enter but makes it necessary for the backdrops to be raised from below instead – a feature found nowhere else in the world. Complex technical machinery is introduced to create the illusion of clouds, thunder, lightning, angels' wings, etc. 124,000 visitors attend 40 performances.

1900 29th Passion Play. Anton Lang's passionate performances as Jesus from 1900–22 greatly influence the Play. The 4,200-seat auditorium is now covered by an iron girder roof-construction with six high arches, open at one end to the stage which remains exposed to the elements. An *Official Book of the Text* is available for the first time. "Oberammergau welcomes guests from around the globe; even three gentlemen from China were seen," reads a newspaper headline. Prominent spectators include crowned heads of state from Russia, France, Sweden, England, Italy, Austria-Hungary, Saxony, Prussia and Denmark, 'unbelievably wealthy Americans' such as Rockefeller and Vanderbilt, 'English sufragettes', Auguste Eiffel, Count Zeppelin, poets, artists, names from the stage, innumerable heads of the church from as far afield as New York and Australia, and Cardinal Ratti, later to become Pope Pius XI. 174,000 spectators.

1910 30th Passion Play. With a total of 223,548 visitors attending 56 performances, the Play proves to be a unique mass spectacle. Visitor structure similar to 1900.

1922 31st Passion Play. The aftermath of World War I results in the Play being postponed by two years. The sculptor Georg Johann Lang (1889–1968) is chosen to direct the Play. Unexpectedly, the number of visitors rises to 311,127, including some 100,000 from abroad.

1930 32nd Passion Play. Modern directive methods are implemented in the new staging by Georg Johann Lang: strictly minimal sets and greater artistic concentration rather than decoration. Instead of an historicised set, a simple, monumental stage is constructed (by the architect Raimund Lang, later mayor of Oberammergau) and the auditorium is extended to seat 5,200. Visitors include the British Prime Minister Sir Ramsay MacDonald, Henry Ford and Rabindranath Tagore.

1934 33rd Passion Play. Special performances on the occasion of the 300th jubilee. Ticket prices and train fares are reduced. The National Socialists call for the motto 'Germany is calling you!' to be added to the posters and an attempt is made to monopolize the 'farmers' play' deriving from the 'blessed power of the earth' for their 'blood and soil' ideology. Some of the people of Oberammergau are taken in by this. Shortly before the general election is held, Hitler takes advantage of Oberammergau's popularity by visiting the village himself. An attempt by Leo Weismantel (1888–1964) to revise the text fails. 440,000 visitors.

1940 The Play is not performed due to the war. Preparations, started in 1938 following a declaration by the Ministry for Propaganda that the Play was 'important to the Reich,' were disbanded.

1950 34th Passion Play. The performances given to an unexpectedly large number of international visitors following the war are used to present the country as one rooted in the western Christian tradition. Prof. Eugen Papst (1886–1956), of Oberammergau, revises and supplements the music, orchestrating it anew. Visitors from the world of politics include the first President of the German Federal Republic, Theodor Heuss, the Chancellor, Konrad Adenauer and the Bavaria Minister President Erhard, as well as Dwight D. Eisenhower, the highest ranking representative of the Allied Forces. 480,000 visitors attend an extended run of 87 performances (33 were planned).

1960 35th Passion Play. Georg Johann Lang, directing the play for the last time, looks for a writer for a contemporary script, but his efforts are in vain. For this reason, the production from 1930 is put on again with very few changes. Both Christian and Jewish critics complain about the negative picture given of Judaism. The Abbot of Ettal, Dr. Johannes Maria Höck, makes minor corrections to the text as a consequence. Approximately 500,000 visitors attend.

1970 36th Passion Play. In 1961, the community of Oberammergau initiates a discussion with theologians and artists with the aim of revising the text that has been changed little since 1870 and the production itself, barely

The executioner's assistants throw dice for Jesus's cloak

modifed since 1930. Carl Orff's suggestion of a return to the Rosner text from 1750 is taken up and rehearsals take place under Hans Schwaighofer who had presented his ideas for staging the Play back in 1966. When the decision is made to use the Daisenberger text again in 1970, Schwaighofer steps down. Anton Preisinger (1912–1989) directs the Lang version. With more than 530,000 visitors attending 102 performances, the conservative fraction feels that its position has been confirmed.

1977 The Rosner trial performances. Attempts to reform the Play continue prior to the next performance. In 1975, the council commissions Schwaighofer to direct a trial performance of the Play using Rosner's text. Schwaighofer devises the stage sets, masks and costumes, Alois Fink the stage adaptation and Wolfgang Fortner, the music. In 1977, 700 actors hold eight performances that are extremely positively received by the public. However, after a local poll is taken, a decision is made against the Rosner text. At first the council is in favour of Rosner, but a newly elected council decides in favour of the Weis/Daisenberger text for the 1980 Play.

1980 37th Passion Play. In 1978 the theologians Leonard Swidler and Gerald Sloyen – on behalf of the Anti-Defamation League – submit suggestions for creating a more positive picture of Judaism. The new director, Hans Maier, takes elements of this criticism into account. He revises Lang's sets for the 1980 production, too. From now on, all 18 leading roles are cast with two performers of equal status. The number of seats is reduced to 4,700. 460,000 people attend.

1984 38th Passion Play. 350th jubilee. Hans Maier makes changes to the texts and sets. Women entitled to perform win the active and passive right to vote on the Passion Play committee. Approximately 480,000 visitors.

1990 39th Passion Play. Although a new generation moves onto the local council in 1984, a decision is made in favour of the Weis/Daisenberger text. This is followed by the election of the youngest ever director of the Play – the 27-year-old sculptor Christian Stückl. A commission responsible for the text, headed by Prof. Rudolf Pesch, works on solutions to the queries raised by the ADL regarding the picture of Judaism portrayed. Following a case taken by three women from Oberammergau to the state court, women are given the same rights to perform in the Play as men. Controversy surrounding the Play leads to permission for a new stage set, among other things, being withdrawn.

Christian Stückl assigns a number of major roles to a younger generation of actors. Together with Otto Huber he returns to Daisenberger's original script and examines the plays held in previous centuries. Certain elements from older plays are re-introduced, such as freezing the action for moments of contemplation ('Ecce Homo', 'Raising of the Cross'). As with the exhibition 'Passion Plays in the Alpine Region', organised together with the 'Haus der Bayerischen Geschichte' (House of Bavarian History), it aims at establishing the Play's position in the present day by analysing exegetical, theological and historical facts associated with the Passion. The text is sensitively revised as is the music (by Markus Zwink). Many of the changes are to ensure that Judaism is appropriately portrayed, both with regard to the symbols used and the costumes. New impulses are gained from a trip to Israel by the principle actors and from meeting major Jewish figures. The performance by the younger generation is positively received. 480,000 visitors.

2000 40th Passion Play. The new political tool – the local referendum – is implemented on issues regarding how best to uphold the village's inheritance. In this way, it is voted in advance that Christian Stückl should remain director of the Play and that Daisenberger's version remain the basis of the text. A decision is also made on the appearance of the façades of the Passion Play Theatre. The council passes a motion to allow those living in Oberammergau who are not Christian to participate. An agreement is made with the Catholic Church that the Archdiocese of Munich-Freising undertakes to become the patron of the Passion Play on the condition that the person appointed approve the production of the Play.

In 1997, the council commissions Christian Stückl with the task of preparing a new production. After a period of stagnation, a younger generation is given the possibility of becoming more closely identified with the Play. Stefan Hageneier, the set and costume designer, conjures up an aesthetically convincing general picture, far removed from the customary image found in films on biblical themes. Work by Christian Stückl and the dramaturg Otto Huber on the texts throws a new light on some of the scenes and figures, allows a dramatic clash to take place between those for and against Jesus, and renders central issues in the Story of the Passion clearer. Markus Zwink composes the music for the new tableaux vivants ('The Feast of Passover', 'God calls Moses from the Burning Bush'), and adapts gems composed by Dedler that were omitted in the past to modifications made to the content of the Play (e.g. 'Moses is Cast out by the Pharaoh').

In 1997/98, the preparatory work is presented to the council and the local clergy, as well as to the theologian, Prof. Ludwig Mödl, appointed by Cardinal Wetter and Bishop von Loewenich. The staging is enthusiastically received by both the public and critics. 500,000 visitors.

2010 41st Passion Play. The council gives the go-ahead for Christian Stückl's new staging. The set designer, Stefan Hageneier, devises an even clearer pictorial language with tableaux vivants in glowing colours. Markus Zwink composes a 'Shema Yisrael' and music for the tableaux vivants, including the new scene 'Moses leads the Israelites through the Red Sea'. Christian Stückl and Otto Huber's reworking of the text results in three largely new scenes, among other changes, at the beginning of the Play and a more condensed, dramatic interrogation scene. Intensive rehearsals contribute towards making the story of Jesus of Nazareth easier to grasp.

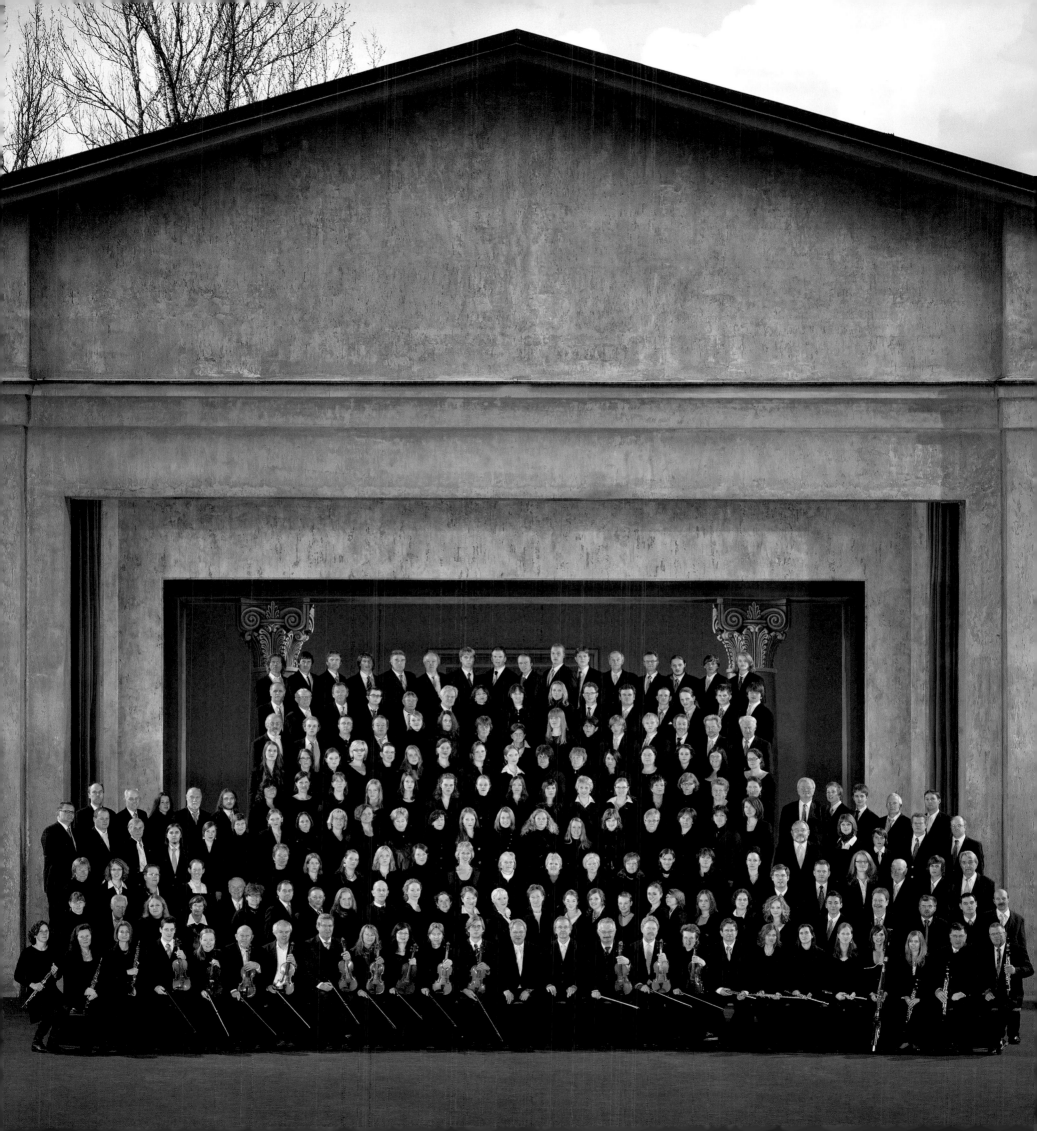

This book has been published to accompany the
41st Oberammergau Passion Play, 15 May–3 October, 2010
Principal Director of the Passion Play: Christian Stückl
Stage-set and costume design: Stefan Hageneier
Deputy Director, Dramatic Adviser and author
of all texts: Otto Huber
Musical Direction: Markus Zwink, Michael Bocklet
Lighting: Martin Feichtner

Photography: Brigitte Maria Mayer
Photographic lighting: Matthias Feldmeier, Martin Feichtner
Post-production: Christian Czech

Edited by the Community of Oberammergau

passion play ²⁰¹⁰
oberammergau

Photographic Credits
All colour plates by Brigitte Maria Mayer, Berlin
pp. 120, 121: Gabriela Neeb (45), Thomas Dashuber (8),
Andrea Göttler (1)
p. 123 left: The Archive of the Archdiocese of Munich and Freising
pp. 123 centre, 124, 125: The Community of Oberammergau Archives
p. 123 right: The Benedictine Abbey, Ettal

© Prestel Verlag, Munich · Berlin · London · New York, 2010
© for all illustrations by the Community of Oberammergau

Front cover: Ecce Homo, Frederick Mayet as Jesus
Back cover: The Last Supper
pp. 2|3: The Entry into Jerusalem
pp. 4: Andreas Richter as Jesus
pp. 5|6: Prologue and Chorus
pp. 127: The Passion Play Chorus and Orchestra, 2010

Prestel Verlag
A member of Verlagsgruppe Random House GmbH

Prestel Verlag
Königinstrasse 9
80539 Munich
Tel. +49 (0)89 24 29 08-300
Fax +49 (0)89 24 29 08-335

www.prestel.de

Prestel Publishing Ltd.
4 Bloomsbury Place
London WC1A 2QA
Tel. +44 (0)20 7323-5004
Fax +44 (0)20 7636-8004

Prestel Publishing
900 Broadway, Suite 603
New York, NY 10003
Tel. +1 (212) 995-2720
Fax +1 (212) 995-2733

www.prestel.com

Library of Congress Control Number is available; British Library
Cataloguing-in-Publication Data: a catalog record for this book is
available from the British Library; Deutsche Nationalbibliothek
holds a record of this publication in the Deutsche National-
bibliografie; detailed bibliographical data can be found under:
http://dnb.d-nb.de

Prestel books are available worldwide. Please contact your
nearest bookseller or one of the above addresses for information
concerning your local distributor.

Translated from the German by Christopher Wynne

Project management: Gabriele Ebbecke
Copy-editing: Christopher Wynne
Design and layout: SOFAROBOTNIK, Augsburg & Munich
Typesetting: Mediengestaltung Vornehm GmbH, Munich
Art direction: Cilly Klotz
Production: Christine Gross
Origination: Reproline Mediateam, Munich
Printing and binding: Mohn media Mohndruck GmbH, Gütersloh

ISBN 978-3-7913-5025-7 (English trade edition)
ISBN 978-3-7913-6280-9 (English edition for Oberammergau)
ISBN 978-3-7913-5024-0 (German trade edition)
ISBN 978-3-7913-6279-3 (German edition for Oberammergau)